31-Day

Purpose *and* Prayer

Devotional

IVETTE CARBONE

PAGE PUBLISHING
Conneaut Lake, PA

First originally published by Page Publishing 2024

ISBN 979-8-89315-290-6 (pbk)
ISBN 979-8-89315-306-4 (digital)

Printed in the United States of America

Day 1

Mitzvah: Share Yeshua's promptings with a friend.

Prayer: Yeshua, you said now I'll listen carefully for your voice and wait to hear whatever you say. Let me hear your promise of peace, the message everyone—your godly lovers—longs to hear.

Today is a beautiful day. I feel inspired to share my heart. This week, I received a text saying that our state park chef was new, and the food was excellent.

I live in a rural area where dining is scarce, and I really appreciated the information she gave me. It may seem unimportant to most people, but I believe these small gestures can change someone's day. In a world where everyone is so busy, we should take time to notice God's promptings.

Write your mitzvah.

Write your prayer.

Day 2

Mitzvah: Give the gift of prayer away.

Prayer: Yeshua, you said that every morning, I must lay out the pieces of my life on the altar and wait for your fire to fall upon my heart.

One of the things that surprises me is that Yeshua will train you even when you don't know it. For most of my married life, I gave myself to working in the ministry.

I worked at the prison ministry and also with women of aglow. I became a pastoral counselor. I wrote my first book. We started a prayer community online, but I never thought I would be leading corporate prayer at my local church.

This has been my greatest joy.

Write your mitzvah.

Write your prayer.

Day 3

Mitzvah: Care for the homeless.

Prayer: Yeshua, you said that I will defend the poor, those who were plundered, the oppressed, the needy who groan for help. I will spring into action to rescue and protect them.

In 2023, the Lord used my younger brother to communicate with me. We were chatting, and he told me that he removed his sneakers and gave them away to a homeless man. It really surprised me. I know this was not a coincidence. So I made a plan to start making snack backpacks. I placed them in my car so that whenever my husband and I spot a homeless person, we give it away. I used to be afraid to get close to them but not anymore. Life is short, and we need to impact the Lord's kingdom. We can easily forget why we are here.

Write your mitzvah.

Write your prayer.

Day 4

Mitzvah: Give your presence away to someone.

Prayer: Yeshua, you said your wraparound presence is my shield. You bring victory to all who are pure in heart.

The truth is that wherever we go, we can give our presence away. Once I learned this, I began to remind myself that it was important not to take this time for granted. Yeshua's needs are very real, and it's so crucial. Tonight, we are heading out to a church concert, and I am not only excited to attend but also excited to be there for others.

You never know what others are suffering. In a world that is so closed off, we have to be willing to step out and give our presence away.

Write your mitzvah.

Write your prayer.

Day 5

Mitzvah: Give the gift of discernment away to someone.

Prayer: Yeshua, in mercy you have seen my troubles, and you have cared for me; even during this crisis in my soul I will be radiant with joy, filled with praise for your love and mercy.

I was sitting one day, watching TV and minding my own business. As I was listening to the church's message on the TV, I heard in my soul as I was looking at the ministers, sensing things were not good. In a few days, my discernment was spot on; it went viral.

As we mature in God, he begins to share more with us. Knowing the truth helps us to pray for the issues at hand. Spiritual gifts shape us to understand things more clearly.

In a world that is so lost, we should try to step back from the mundane of our existence and think about asking God for the gift of discernment.

Write your mitzvah.

Write your prayer.

Day 6

Mitzvah: Give your wisdom away to someone.

Prayer: Yeshua, where can wisdom be found? It is born in the fear of God. Everyone who follows his ways will never lack his living and understanding.

Yeshua is infinite, and we are finite. He shares things with us when we are ready. I know secrets today that I didn't know when I was younger. Today I understand why trauma is so hard to deal with; it's because we need wisdom.

Through wisdom, we are not shaken. If you have a sense of loss, aloneness, isolation, depression, or even suicide, you are not alone. Trauma is not a death sentence. Yes, we have to do the spiritual work if Yeshua does not heal us. But whatever the condition may be, there is always hope. Yeshua can give you the wisdom to help others.

Write your mitzvah.

Write your prayer.

Day 7

Mitzvah: Give your passion away to someone.

Prayer: Lord, with passion, I pursue and cling to you. Because I feel your grip on my life. I keep my soul close to you.

Every Sunday, when our pastor preaches, we cannot deny his passion for the kingdom. Our Wednesday Bible study teacher has an amazing devotion to the Word. Once a month, we attend an end-time class. The Bible teacher also has a great dedication to the Word. If you feel that your journey is getting dry, find a group where there is life. Explore what makes you passionate.

A personality test can help you get started. Speaking to a friend, relative, coach, or mentor will help in the process. My favorite part of the new season in the series *The Chosen* is when Jesus rebukes the Pharisees. It's a great reminder to see the passion of Christ displayed for us.

Write your mitzvah.
Write your prayer.

Day 8

Mitzvah: Leave an inheritance to someone.

Prayer: Yahweh, you alone are my inheritance. You are my prize, my pleasure, and my portion. You hold my destiny and timing in your hands.

This is something most people don't think about, and it is an inheritance. I know so many families that have been so foolish with what God has given them. The secular things of this world are of lower value, and investing in a kingdom inheritance is higher in value. It's so simple, and yet people really don't get it.

Write your mitzvah.

Write your prayer.

Day 9

Mitzvah: Donate your stuff to charity.

Prayer: Yeshua, you said to share freely and give generously to those in need. Their good deeds will be remembered forever. They will have influence and honor.

One of my favorite things to do is to declutter my closets. It can be challenging, and yet I do it very often. It's a great way to give back. I even donated my first book to coffee houses and little libraries in communities. Something so simple can be remembered in eternity.

Write your mitzvah.

Write your prayer.

Day 10

Mitzvah: Share the gift of laughter with someone.

Prayer: Yeshua, our mouths were filled with laughter, our tongues with songs of joy. Life is not only to be braved but to be enjoyed.

In a world with so much chaos, we can give the gift of laughter. Laughter is medicine to the soul. I have been attending our church for seven months. I don't know anyone like our pastor, but he has a way of making us laugh. For a while, I was worried that I would not find this culture of believers on earth. I can honestly say I cannot live without these folks. Thank you, God, for the gift of laughter.

Write your mitzvah.

Write your prayer.

Day 11

Mitzvah: Leave a legacy of a life lived as a soldier.

Prayer: Yeshua, I will sing of your strength. In the morning, I will sing of your love, for you are my fortress and my refuge in times of trouble. You are my strength; I will sing praise to you. God is my fortress, my God on whom I can rely.

This should be the believer's goal. I know that the journey is tough. Navy seals are broken to the point of exhaustion because it prepares them for a military operation from the sea, air, and land. Let's support the kingdom agenda for God. He truly needs us more than we know.

Write your mitzvah.

Write your prayer.

Day 12

Mitzvah: Every minute of the day, I get to do something for Yeshua.

Prayer: Yeshua, every single moment, you are thinking of me. You cherish me constantly in your every thought. Your desires toward me are more than the grains of the sand on every shore. When I wake up, you're still with me.

Meaning and purpose help us to survive our condition. I heard a true story on YouTube of a woman with suicide pain. Her only way not to feel her excruciating pain was to help others in their journey.

There's a true story movie called *Snowbound*. It is about a young couple who was stranded in the mountains. The one thing that kept the wife alive was her diary. She said it was her lifeline.

One last true story is a movie called *Saint Judy*. This woman changed the United States law of asylum and saved countless lives in the process.

Write your mitzvah.

Write your prayer.

Day 13

Mitzvah: No suffering is purposeless.

Prayer: Yeshua, Jesus's suffering and his emotional turmoil while being rejected, betrayed, and crucified.

Suffering is part of the journey. I know for myself when I have prayed for a miracle, and God doesn't answer me.

It can be unsettling. The mutilated scars that believers have had to endure. I'm sure the apostles felt the same way. We will never understand all the atrocities on this side of heaven. God wants to be glorified in everything. Let's live and die for Yeshua.

Write your mitzvah.

Write your prayer.

Day 14

Mitzvah: Give love away. We can all behave like Nazis and can fall short of the glory of God.

Prayer: Yeshua, your love is like a flood overflowing its banks with kindness.

Love is the highest emotion in us. It does matter when we choose to be selfish. God is so romantic to call us his bride. We will never really understand the love he has for us on the side of eternity. It's a free gift to love.

The following are lyrics by Karen Carpenter:

> Funny but it seems I always wind up here with
>   you.
> Nice to know somebody loves me.
> Funny but it seems that it's the only thing to do.
> Run and find the one who loves me.

This song is a prophetic love song to the bride of Christ even though it was written on a secular platform.

Write your mitzvah.

Write your prayer.

Day 15

Mitzvah: Explore God daily.

Prayer: Direct me, Yahweh, throughout my journey so I can experience your plans for my life. Reveal the life paths that are pleasing to you.

It simply means to read his word and to experience the many wonders and rivers of God.

The earth looks like rubbish compared to eternity, so why do we give in to all the noise of this world? This is a great mitzvah because we have to get out of ourselves. That is one reason why I enjoy writing; it puts me in a state of no distractions. I get to reflect on God's thoughts.

Write your mitzvah.

Write your prayer.

Day 16

Mitzvah: Share hope with others. Hope is like dancing in a parade. The potency of the atmosphere is so intoxicating.

Prayer: Yeshua, you're the hope that holds me and the stronghold to shelter me. The only God for me and my great confidence.

A journal is like having a friend. You treasure the time of solitude and reflection. A scrapbook journal with photo cards and quotes is also a great way to give hope to others. Anytime I walk into Barnes and Noble, I sometimes pass by the journals. I love the leather-bound journals because of their vintage look. I keep them on a table just in case I get an inspiration, and I can quickly jot it down. There are many ways to give hope. The Holy Spirit will guide you when you ask him.

Write your mitzvah.

Write your prayer.

Day 17

Mitzvah: Do good. Don't live like the prince of darkness if you want to see heaven.

Prayer: Yeshua, for your goodness and love, pursue me all the days of my life.

The blessing of doing good keeps us from getting depressed. Doing good is like looking at a painting and capturing its beauty. Its fruits are life-giving. It makes life easier when we are not focused on our conditions.

There are countless men and women who have shaken the world for God in different ways. This evil world can corrupt us if we are not spiritually awake.

Write your mitzvah.

Write your prayer.

Day 18

Mitzvah: Listen to worship music. When life feels heavy, lost, or uncertain, sing to Yeshua. Your calling and devotion to God have levels of warfare, and heaven isn't cheap.

Prayer: Yeshua, I would have lost heart unless I had believed that I would see the goodness of the Lord in the land of the living.

I used to take music for granted. But today, it is a part of my walk with Yeshua. Revelation is progressive, so I learned later in life that God sent me songs. It is so exhilarating to know that I am connected to my father through songs. It truly is romantic and a love story to walk with our King.

Write your mitzvah.

Write your prayer.

Day 19

Mitzvah: Stop seeking Yeshua's hand. Only a tiny percentage will make it to heaven.

Prayer: Yeshua, turn my heart toward your stature and not toward selfish gain.

As I rend upon this thought, I know it's true. Many believers just want stuff from God—healing, deliverance a house, and financial security, which are not bad things to pray for. In America, it has become an idol, and it is so saddening.

We were created to go higher and closer to him. Our King is coming, and we don't want to look like a sick bride. The Lord's eyes are like eyes of fire. Let's not take for granted what he requests of us.

Write your mitzvah.

Write your prayer.

Day 20

Mitzvah: Share with a friend your trust in God. When God doesn't heal us right away, it is because we are in process.

Prayer: Yeshua, it is so much better to trust in you to save me than to put my confidence in someone else.

This has been a tough reality for me to accept because our soul is constantly craving relief from a lot of our conditions.

What I have learned is that we are not our own. We have been given the gift of life, and we have a creator who knows all things, and we don't. We are here to glorify him and submit to him.

Write your mitzvah.

Write your prayer.

Day 21

Mitzvah: Don't give up. Life is supposed to be lived by Yeshua's many streams.

Prayer: Yeshua, here's what I've learned through it all: Don't give up and don't be impatient be entwined with the Lord.

We all know we can get distracted by our battles. We need to be reminded that life is not all dread. Try to find the small things that we neglect to appreciate. I love to travel, but I also enjoy simple things like cooking, hosting dinner gatherings, and solitude.

Write a letter to the prince or princess whom Yeshua created. The things of this world will never satisfy him or her because our home is an eternal place.

Write your mitzvah.

Write your prayer.

Day 22

Mitzvah: Share your inner power of faith to a friend; it is indestructible.

Prayer: Great is our Lord and mighty in power.

I know the fear of the Lord is what keeps my faith grounded. The Lord gave me this song: "Count Your Blessings."

> When upon life's billows you are tempest tossed,
> When you are discouraged, thinking all is lost,
> Count your many blessings name them one by one,
> And it will surprise you what the Lord hath done.
>
> Are you ever burdened with a load of care?
> Does the cross seem heavy you are called to bear?
> Count your many blessings, ev'ry doubt will fly,
> And you will be singing as the days go by.
>
> When you look at others with their lands and gold,
> Think that Christ has promised you His wealth
>   untold;
> Count your blessing, money cannot buy
> Your reward in heaven, nor your home on high.
>
> So amid the conflict, whether great or small,
> Do not be discouraged, God is over all;
> Count your many blessings, angels will attend,
> Help and comfort give you to your journey's end.

Write your mitzvah.
Write your prayer.

Day 23

Mitzvah: Find a place of solitude with Yeshua. Our journey with God is an eternal reality.

Prayer: Yeshua, you said, "Be still and know that I am God."

My place of solitude is when I am fasting, I feel the lightest and closest to Yeshua. I feel like I am in a cloud of peace.

I imagine my soul rising higher and higher and drifting into a royal sleep. My bridal dress is not of this world. I am captivated by how beautiful it is. I hear the chants and prayers at the western wall, and Yeshua's glory is too strong to bear. The angels walk to and fro, and I say to myself, "I hope this never ends."

Write your mitzvah.

Write your prayer.

Day 24

Mitzvah: Give thanks to Yeshua. Life is a gift. Before Yeshua created the world and spirit realm, Yeshua was.

Prayer: Yeshua, you said to give thanks to the Lord for he is good, for his steadfast love endures forever.

When I reflect on this, it changes my soul. There is always something to be thankful for. Yeshua does kiss our conditions every day, whether we realize it or not. Yeshua is an ear that can calm our storms. Yeshua is the only one that can wrap you in his arms.

Write your mitzvah.

Write your prayer.

Day 25

Mitzvah: Share with a friend the whispers of God. It brings life, not death.

Prayer: Yeshua, for your whispers in the night, give me wisdom and show me what to do next.

Make friends with a person or a group. This is spiritual healing. It is simple to brush this off. A whisper from God can bring healing to your soul. The Holy Spirit truly wants to help us in the healing process.

Write your mitzvah.

Write your prayer.

Day 26

Mitzvah: Share with a friend the idols of self (distractions) that need to be eradicated.

Prayer: Yeshua, you said those who cling to worthless idols turn away from God's love for them.

The carnal soul cannot survive in an empty world; it needs God. If we indulge and feed on ourselves, it only brings death. It's God's light in us that brings life.

Write your mitzvah.

Write your prayer.

Day 27

Mitzvah: Share with a friend the awe and the mysteries of God together.

Prayer: Yeshua, you said the whole earth is filled with awe at your wonders. Where morning dawns and evening fades, you call forth songs of joy.

There is nothing more exciting than to share Yeshua's mysteries with a friend. I have learned more about Yeshua for decades when shared with others.

Write your mitzvah.

Write your prayer.

Day 28

Mitzvah: Do something outside of your comfort zone with a friend. We are not ordinary.

Prayer: Yeshua, you said the steps of a man are ordered by the Lord who takes delight in his journey.

My spiritual life has been extremely strange, but I have learned to accept it. Let the Holy Spirit lead you.

Write your mitzvah.

Write your prayer.

Day 29

Mitzvah: Share with a friend your angel encounters if the Lord permits. A human soul is much greater than an angel.

Prayer: Yeshua, you said God sends angels with special orders to protect us wherever we go, defending us from all harm.

My first encounter: I saw an angel standing in my hallway in New Jersey. He was a young teenager.

He was looking at himself in the mirror. I didn't know it at the time because he looked like a real person. But later, I found out that no one had ever seen this teenager in the building. God is mysterious.

Write your mitzvah.

Write your prayer.

Day 30

Mitzvah: Find someone who is more desperate for God than you. Spiritual hunger is deeper than intelligence.

Prayer: Yeshua, you said that truth's shining light will guide me in my choices and decisions. The revelation of your Word makes my pathway clear.

What I have learned is that when you have the right people around you, it can make a big difference in your spiritual journey. Hungry people for God are attractive. Anointed men and women of God can change your life forever.

Write your mitzvah.

Write your prayer.

Day 31

Mitzvah: Action speaks louder than words. Nothing happens by chance.

Prayer: Yeshua, you said to be brave and courageous and never lose hope. Yes, keep on waiting, for he will never disappoint you!

We have to be in a relationship with God in order to get things done for his kingdom. Don't listen to the naysayers. His grace is amazing! The following are lyrics by Karen Carpenter:

> We've only just begun to live…
> Before the risin' sun we fly,
> So many roads to choose,
> We start out walking and learn to run.

Write your mitzvah.
Write your prayer.

About the Author

Ivette Carbone is an author and ordained pastoral counselor. She has a master's degree in biblical counseling. She and her husband lead corporate prayer at their local church. She also leads a community prayer online. She loves to travel. She likes to host dinner gatherings at her home. She and her husband reside in South Carolina. She has a stepson and two grandchildren.